WELCOME TO THE SAFARI PARK

THE SAN DIEGO ZOO SAFARI PARK IS AN ADVENTURE like no other. Here, trails and vistas reveal memorable views of lions lounging in the grass, antelope and giraffes mingling on the savannas, and rhinos wallowing in water holes. Full of animal encounters and fun experiences, the Park is one of the most distinctive and successful wildlife preserves in the world—a unique place where guests can be immersed in the natural world and make powerful and lasting connections with wildlife.

Since 1972, the Safari Park has worked to care for the world's wildlife and to engage the public. We hope you, too, will enjoy the Park's offerings and follow the sentiment that was expressed on its opening day:

Join us here … to contemplate the wild animals of the world and nature's wilderness … to strengthen a commitment to wildlife conservation throughout the world, and to strive toward man's own survival through the preservation of nature.

SAN DIEGO ZOO®

SAFARI PARK

OFFICIAL GUIDEBOOK

The Swahili word for lion, *simba*, also means "king," "strong," and "aggressive."

CONTENTS

ABOUT THE SAFARI PARK

Other animals often congregate near giraffes, whose height enables them to see predators from a distance on the African plains—and the food trucks at the Safari Park.

ABOUT THE SAFARI PARK

THE SAFARI PARK IS AN EXPANSIVE WILDLIFE SANCTUARY, home to more than 3,000 animals representing over 300 species. Its renowned botanical collection represents 3,500 species and 1.75 million specimens. Nearly half of the Park's 1,800 acres have been set aside as a protected native species habitat.

The Park was the brainchild of Charles Schroeder, D.V.M, director of the San Diego Zoo from 1953 to 1973. Envisioning a "zoo of the future" with greater space for the animals, he worked to create a haven for wild animals in zoos and to raise awareness about the crisis of vanishing species and the importance of the conservation efforts necessary to protect them. More than 18,000 mammals and 8,000 birds have been born and hatched at the Park since it opened.

The Safari Park was originally conceived as a "back country animal preserve" that would be dedicated to breeding and maintaining species so that animals would not have to be collected from the wild. As the concept developed, however, it became clear that the Park could be both a preserve and a site for visitors to enjoy. More than 15 years in the making, the Safari Park was officially dedicated on May 9, 1972.

For more than 45 years, the Safari Park—previously known as the San Diego Wild Animal Park—has cared for rare and exotic animals from around the world.

In addition to exhibits, safaris, and shows, the Safari Park offers keeper talks and animal encounters with cheetahs, aardvarks, servals, and other exotic and rare species.

Strollers, lockers, and motorized wheelchairs are available for rent on a first-come, first-served basis near the entrance.

A map highlighting the most accessible walkways also marks the stops for the Park's courtesy shuttle. These maps are available at the Park's ticket booths and at Ranger Base.

Guests who have difficulty standing in line or who have limited mobility may request an "Easy Access Pass" at any ticket window at the entrance to the Safari Park, Ranger Base, or at the Africa Tram. This pass allows guests with a disability—and three additional members of their party— to be directed to a designated boarding area.

The Park can provide visitors who are deaf or hard of hearing with scripted information for shows or tours. These scripts can be picked up at Guest Services or at Ranger Base. If guests would like an ASL Interpreter, the Park requests a minimum of one week's notice.

Guests with disabilities may bring their trained service animal (dog or miniature horse). Pets, companion animals, comfort animals, and animals in training are not allowed entry. Service animals must be under control of their handler at all times. Visitors may kennel their service animal during their visit. Restricted areas can be found on the Safari Park's Service Animal Map.

The Park is accessible to guests using manual and electric wheelchairs and certain nontraditional wheelchairs and mobility devices. If a child is using a stroller as an accessibility device and is unable to transfer out of it, visitors may request a "wheelchair tag" from the Guest Services Center.

Shuttle service is available for access to different locations around the Safari Park. Please download and refer to the Map for Guests with Disabilities, which shows the ADA (Americans with Disabilities Act) Shuttle stops in the Safari Park. The shuttle service runs on a continuous route throughout the day.

There is no smoking on the grounds of the San Diego Zoo Safari Park.

Founded as a haven for rare and endangered animals in 1972, the Safari Park is a world-renowned wildlife conservancy and botanical garden.

The Africa Tram provides a closer look at the Park's African wildlife. As the tram winds through some of the Park's large field habitats, a guide will point out particular animals and describe interesting behaviors. Many animal favorites are seen here, including giraffes, rhinos, gazelles, and antelope. There are also ostriches, African crowned cranes, and other birds mingling with the mammals. Many interactions happen around a large watering hole, where the different species come together. Across the bridge and around the bend, visitors will see some of the most beautiful views in the Park. As the tram returns to the station, guests may even pass a lion or two resting on the hillside. When the journey is over, there's still more of Africa to explore throughout the Park!

Both male and female giraffes have two distinct, hairy horns called ossicones.

The Behind-the-Scenes Safari offers guests a one-of-a-kind look at off-exhibit areas inaccessible to the general public. Guests are escorted on a small electric cart by an experienced guide, who provides the inside scoop on the Safari Park's animal collection and conservation work.

There are several Behind-the-Scenes Safaris for guests ages three and older (unless otherwise stated). Guests can view the animals' night-time bedrooms, learn about the amazing work the animal keepers do, get an up-close visit with one of the Animal Ambassadors, or possibly offer a treat to an okapi. They can view the Safari Park's state-of-the-art veterinary center, travel "down under" to visit some Aussie mates at Walkabout Australia, or learn about the world-class conservation taking place at the Nakita Kahn Rhino Rescue Center. The Behind-the-Scenes Safari is the best way to get an insider's view of the Safari Park.

The Caravan Safari allows guests to adventure directly into the Park's expansive Asian and African field habitats on the back of a flatbed truck. Experienced guides interpret animal behavior and entertain guests with conservation stories. There is often an opportunity to feed a rhino or giraffe and frequent chances to capture incredible photos of wildlife.

The Caravan Safari has several caravans to choose from, including one for kids. Each caravan visits several field exhibits and provides an opportunity to feed giraffes.

Roar & Snore enables visitors to experience safari camping without having to travel to Africa. The campground overlooks the African Plains field habitat, where giraffes, rhinos, antelope, gazelles, and many other animals roam. Guests slumber to the rumblings of lions and elephants and wake up to the morning courtship calls of African crowned cranes.

Roar & Snore Safari sleepovers are offered most of the year in a variety of themed programs, including ones for adults, families, Girl Scouts, and schools. Sleepovers include tent accommodations, camp activities, an after-hours look at the wild lives of the Park's animals, guided walks, a campfire program, a delicious dinner and hot breakfast, and the opportunity to experience the Safari Park at night.

Roar & Snore guests can enjoy a view of the Safari Park's African elephant herd.

During a Cart Safari, guests can observe herds of giraffes, rhinos, antelope, gazelles, and more in a natural setting while a knowledgeable guide explains the Park's history and answers questions about the animals and their care. From the comfort of a safari cart, visitors will learn how to read animal behavior, gain insight into animal adaptations, and find out what makes each animal unique. The relaxed pace allows for photo stops as well as opportunities to watch a keeper offer an enrichment item or treat to the wildlife in the field enclosure. Two Cart Safaris are offered: one focuses on the African animals, while the other focuses on the Asian animals.

Visitors on a Cart Safari will learn conservation facts about the Park's African or Asian animals from their tour guide.

Flightline Safari

The Flightline Safari is perfect for those guests looking for an exhilarating, wind-in-your-face thrill. During this safari, participants soar like condors from a ridgetop and glide two-thirds of a mile over open exhibits filled with exotic animals. Professional staff will provide training and a short practice flight before taking guests up to the main line overlooking the picturesque San Pasqual Valley. Age and safety restrictions apply for the Flightline Safari.

Guests on the Flightline Safari will soar as high as 160 feet above the ground with rhinos, deer, and other animals in the fields below.

Adventure seekers can climb, balance, swing, and walk through the trees on the Safari Park's Jungle Ropes Safari, challenging themselves with a daring experience that offers unique trails to test one's "jungle" skills. There are rope bridges to cross, aerial tightropes to navigate, swinging log steps to negotiate, and moving platforms to cross, among many other thrills.

During their adventure, guests can travel through the trails at their own pace, with staff available for assistance if necessary. There are three trails to choose from, with each offering a different challenge. Participants will put on a safety harness and be given instruction by trained staff prior to entering the trail—then it's up to them to make like a monkey and swing!

Each route in the Jungle Ropes Safari has about 12 elements of balance and daring.

Shiley's Cheetah Run, located near Lion Camp, features a cheetah running on a straight 330-foot-long track that allows it to reach speeds approaching 70 miles per hour.

The Cheetah Safari offers reserved trackside seating where guests can watch from just feet away as the cheetah whooshes by in pursuit of a mechanical lure. Before the cat makes its entrance, safari guests get an up-close encounter with another African animal. After the cheetah has finished its sprint, the cat and its trainer come over for an exclusive meet-and-greet. Cheetah Safari is available only through advance registration, and space is limited.

Cheetah Run provides guests with the opportunity to take photos of a cheetah interacting with its trainer.

VIP This safari is the ultimate way to experience the Park, enabling guests to tour off-exhibit areas, interact with animals, and receive the best in personalized service.

The Park's team of professionals customize each Ultimate Safari to suit the needs and interests of the participants, whether they are seeking a thrilling adventure, looking to journey to some of the most exclusive areas of the Park, or hoping to get up close with animal ambassadors. Visitors can spend up to eight hours exploring the Safari Park with a personal tour guide. Advance reservations are required.

Guests who choose the Ultimate Safari receive extended time with a tour guide who provides fascinating facts and conservation updates about the Park's rare and endangered animals.

Guests can request to visit with the Park's elephant herd behind-the-scenes during their Ultimate Safari.

SAFARI BASE CAMP

African thorn trees like this one help create ambiance at the Park and also provide resting spots for lions, antelope, and visitors. This particular tree is the largest of its kind in the United States.

SAFARI BASE CAMP

SAFARI BASE CAMP IS LOCATED JUST BEYOND THE PARK'S entrance portal. A 70-foot-tall African thorn tree greets visitors as they enter the main plaza of Base Camp. This tree came from one of the Park's first horticulturists, who spent two months in Africa, studying and gathering plants for landscaping. The Park's horticulturists propagated the seeds he brought back and planted the sapling at Thorntree Terrace, where it remains today.

Safari Base Camp offers shops, restaurants, animal habitats, presentation areas, and activities such as the Conservation Carousel for children.

Chilean flamingos live in a lagoon at Safari Base Camp. They are the largest of the world's six flamingo species.

Wings of the World aviary is located near the Park's entrance and is on the way to Safari Base Camp. Some species in the aviary are rare in the wild, and others are seldom seen in collections. There are no moats or barriers. People could actually reach out and touch the birds—if the birds would let them.

Everything in the aviary is designed to approximate the birds' natural habitat, from the concrete footpath that resembles the color and texture of dried mud, to the rock outcroppings and waterfalls that spill into the marshes where the shorebirds strut. Terrestrial, midlevel, and upper canopies of vegetation provide a variety of habitats for the birds to nest and forage. Between the spoonbills, ibises, hammerkops, and Storm's storks, there's always something new to see.

Storm's storks are the second rarest storks in the world. The Safari Park was the first zoo outside of Asia to breed this species.

Guests can get face-to-face with some of the Safari Park's friendlier animals—like this serval—at the Animal Ambassador Stage.

Meerkats may look like prairie dogs on a diet, but they are actually related to the mongoose. They often dig in the dirt looking for insects to eat, or spend time adding to their extensive underground burrows. These little carnivores live and work together in a group called a gang or a mob. They work for the common good, whether helping to care for youngsters or looking out for danger.

Meerkats on lookout duty balance on their hind legs. A meerkat sentry doesn't miss much. If trouble is spotted, the lookout alerts the others, and they all dash back into the safety of their burrows. When they're not on duty, they relax on their backside with their front paws draped across their stomach.

The Park's group of meerkats—all females!—came from the Zoo in 2009. The Park participates in the Species Survival Plan (SSP) for meerkats and is waiting to receive a male through the program.

BEHIND THE SCENES

To the untrained eye, all meerkats look the same, but the keepers at the Park know their distinct personality traits. Some are shy, while others are dominant, edging the others out for the first bite of enrichment food. The meerkats at the Park are intelligent and food-motivated. They love enrichment—especially puzzle feeders—and are always curious about new items. Because of the meerkats' daily training program, they willingly get on a scale once a month to be weighed.

Meerkats balance on their long, stiff tail, which they use like a kickstand on a bicycle.

The Park's one-ton bronze rhino measures nearly 13 feet long. The statue was commissioned in honor of Anderson Borthwick, who arranged to send 18 southern white rhinos from Africa to create a breeding herd at the Safari Park.

Relatives of raccoons, coatimundis from South America are active, social animals.

Kangaroos are able to keep hopping without expending much energy. In fact, they actually burn less energy the faster they hop.

DID YOU KNOW?

Large kangaroos can cover 23 feet in one hop when cruising at top speed and have been clocked at 30 miles per hour in short bursts!

WALKABOUT AUSTRALIA IS DESIGNED to represent Australia's rural landscapes and the animals, plants, and signs of human habitation encountered along backcountry roads. In this time of changing climate conditions, Australia—like California—is experiencing longer and more widespread periods of drought, along with an increase in wildfires. Water is a more precious resource than ever, and Walkabout Australia explores that vital connection.

Along the way, visitors encounter four habitats: kangaroos and wallabies grazing in a savanna grassland; ducks and geese paddling through wetlands; kangaroos climbing trees and birds stalking on the ground in a rain forest; and water-wise plants in a desertscape. The landscape is dotted with features like a windmill and a water tank, and it all leads to and through Zuest Station. Modeled after the sheep shearing sheds of Australia, the station shows visitors the process of making wool textiles, from fleece to fabric.

Magpie geese live in large flocks and are a regular sight in wetland habitats.

DID YOU KNOW?

A female kangaroo is called a doe, flyer, jill, or roo; a male is called a buck, boomer, jack, or old man.

Kangaroos are marsupials—meaning that the females raise their joeys in a pouch. In addition to their powerful legs, kangaroos have a thick, strong tail that helps them hop. Their tail serves with their feet as a tripod to lean back and rest on. Kangaroos are social, gathering in groups called a mob, usually made up of a dominant male and females with their young. They have acute hearing and vision, which helps them to keep watch for potential predators.

Wallabies are smaller versions of their kangaroo relatives—except wallabies eat more leaves, so they have flatter molars. About three feet tall and 40 pounds, wallabies are agile, curious, and active, mostly in the morning and evening. Walkabout Australia's wallabies have the distinction of being red-necked with a rusty red flourish across their shoulders and rump.

Tree kangaroos have adaptations that allow them to spend their lives in trees. They have long, sharp claws for climbing, and instead of hopping, they use their strong legs and tail to leap and balance in the treetops. They can leap as far as 30 feet from tree to tree. Tree kangaroos sleep 60 percent of the time, curling up in whatever tree they happen to be in. Since they are mostly solitary, they ignore one another, even if they're sharing the same tree.

Tree kangaroos are the only kangaroos that can move their back legs independently of one another and move backward, which is how they climb down a tree.

All three cassowary species have a casque, also called a helmet, that starts to develop on top of their head at one to two years of age.

These birds are elusive and mysterious yet also famous for their ferocity. Tall, crested, and prehistoric looking, flightless cassowaries stalk through the forest underbrush looking for fruit and fungi. With a specialized digestive system, they can eat things that would be poisonous to other animals.

CATCH A GLIMPSE

Walkabout Australia is home to numerous birds, including magpie geese, freckled ducks, rajah shelducks, and Australian brush turkeys. Keep an eye out for these avian Aussies as you wander!

Cassowaries are shaped just right to crash through brush in a hurry—but if cornered, they can display the characteristic that gives them their fierce nickname, "the most dangerous bird in the world." Cassowaries have an elongated and razor-sharp claw on each foot that can slice an impressive gash in any potential predator, including a human!

ELEPHANT VALLEY

The largest elephant on record was an adult male African elephant weighing 24,000 pounds.

ELEPHANT VALLEY

ELEPHANT VALLEY IS HOME TO THE PARK'S AFRICAN ELEPHANT HERD and Tembo Stadium, where various presentations take place throughout the year. Covering more than five and a half acres, the elephant habitat includes two swimming areas and two barns where the elephants can warm up during the winter months if needed.

The Elephant Overlook is an elevated walking path that leads visitors along the side of the habitat to see what the Park's pachyderms are up to. From the Overlook is a view of the elephant barns and holding yards. The elephants go to the holding yards in the mornings when the keepers are cleaning the spacious main yards and hiding treats for them to discover. The Elephant Viewing Patio, located at the south end of Elephant Valley, provides a great view of the main yards, where the elephants forage for their treats. The patio also offers the best view of the pond—where the elephants love to get wet!

Elephant calves are hairy, with a long tail and short trunk. At birth, they stand about three feet tall.

CATCH A GLIMPSE

To see more of the Park's African herd, watch the high-definition Elephant Cam (sdzsafaripark.org/elephant-cam).

The African elephant herd at the Safari Park includes adults that were rescued from Swaziland in 2003. The elephants were scheduled to be culled due to overpopulation. One of the females was pregnant and gave birth to a son in 2004. Since then, the Park has celebrated many new additions.

Newborns have a 21- to 22-month gestation period and weigh a hefty 200 to 270 pounds at birth. Calves stick close to their mother and nurse frequently. The rest of the herd nurtures the calves, too, forming protective circles when they get spooked by new noises or scents.

African elephants have ears that are shaped like the continent of Africa. They flap their ears on hot days to cool down.

Although an elephant's skin can be up to one inch thick, it is so sensitive that the animal can feel a fly landing on its back.

Elephants are affectionate and form strong bonds that are reinforced by behaviors such as sparring and trunk touching. At the Safari Park, the herd is large and varied—making for interesting group dynamics. Calves "inherit" their mother's status within the herd. Bottom ranked animals are submissive to their elders and the other calves that outrank them. Instead of walking head-on into a dominant group of elephants, for example, lower-ranking elephants will turn around and back into the space. They'll also get out of the way when a more dominant elephant is moving around. Elephants must obey the social rules or risk upsetting their 6,500-pound superiors!

Elephant herds are led by an older, experienced female called a matriarch, who decides when and where the herd will eat, travel, and rest.

Elephant Viewing Patio

Late each morning, the elephants enthusiastically rush into the main yard to find treats and enrichment items that keepers have placed around the yard. The Elephant Viewing Patio offers a great view of all the action, and staff members are on hand to point out individual elephants and share information about their personality. It is also the best place to watch the pachyderms playing in their pool!

MISSION CONSERVATION

The Park's elephant keepers have an ongoing collaboration with staff at the San Diego Zoo Institute for Conservation Research to ensure the elephants' well-being and sustainability. Using specially designed elephant collars that incorporate GPS and audio recording technology, they can document the elephants' behavior 24 hours a day.

The keepers have also trained a male at the Park to mount a custom-made model elephant so they can collect his semen and provide it to other zoos. In addition, Park keepers have trained the female elephants to enter a clean holding area and urinate. From those urine samples, Park staff have been able to conduct hormone tests to learn more about the females' reproductive cycles, determine conception dates, and anticipate the birth of calves.

Elephants have over 40,000 muscles in their trunk—more than humans have in their entire body.

SAFARI NOTES

Female African elephants emit "rumble" calls that travel long distances, broadcasting to potential suitors that they are approaching the start of their breeding season. Their calls are so low in frequency, however, that only one-third of the sound can be heard by human ears.

WORLD GARDENS

The Baja Garden is home to the largest collection of rare boojum trees outside their native habitat in Mexico.

WORLD GARDENS

THE SAFARI PARK, AN ACCREDITED BOTANICAL GARDEN, features a variety of flora, much of it found in the Park's World Gardens. This territory includes the Conifer Arboretum, Baja Garden, Old World Succulent Garden, and Nativescapes Garden, as well as the Bonsai Pavilion and Epiphyllum Trail.

Over the years, the Safari Park has been able to maintain plants that represent geographical areas all over the world by working with local garden clubs, botanical societies, and specialty nurseries. It also receives plant specimens from other countries through special permits. The Park's location and its varied elevations enable it to sustain a wide variety of plants, creating a collection that few places in the world could duplicate.

The iridescent blooms of epiphyllums are a dazzling but short-lived visual treat each spring.

Bonsai Pavilion

Bonsai, which means "tree planted in a tray," has been a popular hobby and art form among gardeners since the late 1880s, when it was first displayed outside China and Japan. Bonsai trees are as varied as they are old. Some stand straight and regal, while others show signs of age and weather.

The Safari Park has housed a bonsai collection since 1982, with arrangements donated and maintained by the San Diego Bonsai Club. In May 2011, the Park opened the new Bonsai Pavilion. The peaceful pavilion features a pond, waterfall, and benches. Notable trees include a 100-year-old California buckwheat and a grapevine brought to the U.S. as a cutting from Italy. At 30,000 square feet, the Bonsai Pavilion has about 20 different species and more than 40 specimens—one of the largest displays in the United States.

Bonsai trees develop masses of fine "feeder roots," which help them take in water and nutrients.

Nativescapes Garden

The Safari Park's Nativescapes Garden features more than 1,500 individual plants representing 500 species. The four-acre garden represents Southern California's diverse plant communities: chaparral, coastal sage scrub, cypress, desert transition, high desert, island, low desert, montane, palm oasis, and riparian.

MISSION CONSERVATION

Plants are the backbone of a healthy ecosystem. They are ecologically linked to wildlife, providing shade, food, and shelter materials. San Diego Zoo Global (SDZG) partners with the Center for Plant Conservation, which is nationally headquartered on-site at the Safari Park to save and protect imperiled plants worldwide.

San Diego County—which has the highest number of endangered plant species of any county in the continental United States—is considered a biodiversity hotspot. SDZG's Native Plant Seed Bank project is helping to conserve local plants by having scientists collect seeds from native flora and freezing them for future use. The seeds can be used for habitat restoration and long-term conservation efforts.

Epiphyllum Trail

CATCH A GLIMPSE
Visit the Epiphyllum Trail
during the month of May to
see the cacti at their
blooming best.

Epiphyllums are members of the cactus family that grow attached to trees in moist climates. They don't harm their host, instead getting nourishment from the air and rain. Each spring, they bloom with flowers—some 10 inches across—that reveal a vivid array of iridescent colors. Epiphyllums are easy to grow. Plants and cuttings are available for purchase at the Plant Trader shop in Safari Base Camp. All plants have been donated and are maintained by members of the San Diego Epiphyllum Society.

Baja Garden

With more than 85 Baja varieties and 150 species of rare plants, the Safari Park's Baja Garden exhibits the world's largest collection of cactus and succulents outside Mexico. These plants were gathered from Mexico via permit in the early 1980s, before the country permanently closed its borders to collectors. Today, the garden showcases extraordinary species like the coastal agave, elephant tree, and the old man cactus. The Baja Garden also has more than 200 boojums—tree-like succulents that have a water-storing trunk and an array of spiny branches with tiny leaves. This collection of boojums is the largest one outside Mexico. Boojums can reach heights of 50 to 60 feet and live to be 250 years old.

The Baja Garden has a wide variety of species with fleshy, water-storing leaves and stems and other drought-tolerant plants.

Old World Succulent Garden

The Safari Park's Old World Succulent Garden shows off the diversity of succulents, representing more than 200 species. Succulents come in an amazing array of shapes and sizes, from 30-foot trees to tiny rosettes just one inch across. A succulent is defined as a plant that stores water in its tissues and structures. Usually the leaves or stems are modified for this storage, but sometimes the root is enlarged. When most people think of succulents, they think of cacti, but many plant species have developed succulent forms to cope with arid environments. These include members of the lily family, some African cycads, and members of the euphorbia family, such as the succulent grape.

DID YOU KNOW?

The Park's plant collection contains more than 3,500 species represented by 1,750,000 specimens. Many of the plants are quite rare and/or endangered.

As a result of efforts by the Safari Park and other organizations, the California condor is coming back from the brink of extinction. The Condor Cam allows people from around the world to watch these birds in real time (sdzsafaripark.org/condor-cam).

CONDOR RIDGE

CONDOR RIDGE CELEBRATES THE DIVERSITY of North America and the animals that are unique to it. The continent's largest flying birds, California condors fly among the boulders and cliffs inside their large aviary. Other animals, such as desert bighorn sheep, Harris' hawks, and brilliant green thick-billed parrots, can also be seen and heard.

Condor Ridge is accessible via Condor Trail or through the new Walkabout Australia habitat. Nearby is a majestic bald eagle, and farther along the path are hawk-headed parrots, toco toucans, ocelots, and burrowing owls. At the end of the trail is an observation deck with an interpretive center that focuses on recovery efforts for desert bighorn sheep and California condors.

The observation deck and interpretive center at Condor Ridge gives visitors information about recent conservation efforts. Although much has been accomplished, condors still need careful protection to survive into the future.

BEHIND THE SCENES

At the off-exhibit Condor Breeding Facility, the keepers sometimes use condor puppets to feed the chicks. Using hand puppets helps limit human contact and lessens the chances of the baby condors imprinting on people. The keepers also use artificial condor eggs to give inexperienced birds practice in caring for an egg. (The condors can't tell the difference between a real egg and an artificial one.)

Native American tribes have great respect for California condors and see them as symbols of power. In legends, condors were called "thunder-birds," because they were thought to bring thunder to the skies with the beating of their huge wings.

When they fly, California condors are a wonderful sight to behold. Their impressive wings catch thermal air currents that rise up as the sun heats the ground. They can stay aloft for hours, soaring through the skies as they scan the grounds below, looking for food.

Like all vultures, California condors feed on dead animals such as deer, cattle, and sheep as well as rodents, rabbits, and fish. As scavengers, they are part of nature's cleanup crew and an important part of the ecosystem.

The bald head and neck of California condors are perfectly designed to keep rotting food from sticking to them as they eat.

Desert Bighorn Sheep

Desert bighorn sheep are amazing climbers and can live in some of the world's steepest, most forbidding habitats. Their current range in the United States is from the San Jacinto Mountains near Palm Springs, California, to the the U.S.-Mexico border. These sheep walk on their third and fourth toes. The bottoms of their feet are very soft, allowing them to easily grip rocks.

Desert bighorn sheep have horns that are made of a bony core and encased in a hard material made largely of keratin, just like our hair and fingernails. Unlike a deer's antlers, which are shed each year, horns are permanently attached. The older an animal gets, the larger its horns grow. Males have larger horns than females.

Male desert bighorn sheep use their horns in head-butting clashes that get more intense during the breeding season. Younger males may pick more fights, but the older males have bigger and stronger horns and can win fairly quickly. The winner usually breeds with all the females; the rest of the males return to bachelor herds or remain solitary until the next breeding season.

MISSION CONSERVATION

The California condor has been one of San Diego Zoo Global's most successful breeding and reintroduction programs. Through partnerships with various organizations, San Diego Zoo Global has helped these birds to thrive once again. In the late 1980s, California condors were extinct in the wild and only 22 were left in zoos. Today, their population numbers nearly 500 with just under 300 flying free in the wild in California, Arizona, Utah, and Baja California, Mexico.

Bald eagles live near bodies of water to be close to their favorite food—fish! When fish are scarce, they will hunt rabbits, squirrels, other birds, and even young deer. They have also been known to steal food from other birds.

It is believed that bald eagles mate for life. Males and females perform special courtship dances in the sky, locking on to each other's talons and tumbling and twisting in the air. Then, just before reaching the ground, they let go.

Bald eagles make large nests high in sturdy trees, or sometimes on the ground if necessary. They return to their nest year after year, adding more twigs, grass, moss, feathers, and branches. Females will lay one to three eggs, and both parents take turns keeping the eggs warm until they hatch. Mothers lay their eggs several days apart, once a year.

Bald eagles are at the top of the food chain; they have no natural enemies. So when their population drops, that means humans have done something to harm their wild habitat. In the mid-20th century, farmers began using pesticides to protect their crops from insects. When the eagles ate fish from bodies of water that had been contaminated by the poison, they became endangered. Fortunately, the use of pesticides is better regulated now, and bald eagles have made a dramatic comeback in some states. This once endangered species has recovered and is now considered threatened.

SAFARI NOTES

Life is a challenge for young eagles: Many don't survive their first year. Usually, the first chick to hatch gets a head start on growth over its siblings, and the biggest eaglet will usually consume most of the food delivered by its parents. This survival strategy ensures that at least one chick will get a good chance at living to adulthood.

Found in North and South America, the burrowing owl is tiny—about 10 inches tall. These owls nest in burrows made by prairie dogs and squirrels, and they hunt throughout the day, especially when raising their young. They also like to bask in the sun, making them easy to observe. They can be surprisingly bold and approachable but often take flight when humans get too close.

These owls like to adorn the entrances of their burrows with dung, animal parts, bottle caps, and other shiny trash. This behavior is thought to attract insects or signal to other birds that the burrow is occupied.

During the day, burrowing owls can see 10 times better than people; at night, they can see 100 times better! Burrowing owls also possess the gift of completely silent flight: the edges of their flight feathers are slightly frayed, allowing the wind to pass through them without making a sound.

MISSION CONSERVATION

Burrowing owls are in decline in California and have nearly vanished along the coast. San Diego Zoo Global is involved

with a burrowing owl conservation program that helps the birds find more long-term homes. In the program, ground squirrels dig burrows for the owls in three different sites across San Diego County. "Burrow cams" will be installed in some underground nests to document how the growing chicks develop.

Ocelots range from southern Texas to northern Argentina in South America. These small cats used to be found throughout Texas and east to Arkansas and Louisiana, but due to overhunting and habitat loss, they are now very rare in the United States.

Like all small cats, ocelots have good vision and hearing, and their long whiskers help them feel their way around. Ocelots spend most of their time on the ground but are good climbers, jumpers, and swimmers. They are most active at night, preying on rodents, birds, snakes, lizards, baby peccaries, young deer, rabbits, and fish.

Historically, ocelots were hunted for their skin. People used to pay more for an ocelot coat—often comprised of 25 ocelot skins—than they did for a car. For more than 30 years, it has been illegal to bring ocelots or their skins into the United States and other countries. Ocelots are not hunted as much as they used to be, but in many areas they are losing their homes when people clear the land of brush. Without places to hide, ocelots cannot survive, because they hunt by ambushing their prey.

SAFARI NOTES

Ocelots are an endangered species that are only active at night, and they are very secretive. They prefer to live in areas with thick vegetation. Ocelots have a special layer on the inside of their eyes that collects light, enabling them to see much better in the dark than people can. During the day, they sleep hidden among bushes, on tree branches, or inside hollow trees.

SAFARI NOTES

Thick-billed parrots are intelligent, curious, and social, living together in flocks up to 1,000 birds. Within the flock, there is a particular "pecking order"—and lots of noise. Their calls sound like children laughing, and they will alert one another if predators are near. Thick-billed parrots seem unbothered by people, even when they are caught, measured, sampled, and released for research purposes.

Thick-billed parrots, which live in the pine forests of northern Mexico, are powerful flyers that can usually escape larger birds of prey. Their seasonal migrations can cover hundreds of miles—and researchers believe they can make the trip in one nonstop flight!

Thick-billed parrots primarily eat pine seeds, perching on one thick, strong foot while using the other to hold and turn the pinecone. To get at the seeds, they shred the pinecone with their beak, starting at the base and removing each seed as they work their way to the tip of the cone in a spiral fashion. Pine seeds are such an important part of their diet that their breeding cycle matches peak pine seed production.

The thick-billed parrot population has dropped since the early 1900s. Hunting and logging in the parrots' pine forest habitat and the illegal capture of birds for the pet trade are the greatest threats facing them. Today, conservationists have established a breeding program and habitat protection plan to ensure the survival of this endangered species.

ASIAN SAVANNA

The notches on the edges of this barasingha deer's ears help keepers to identify it from others in the herd. The location of each notch corresponds to a number.

DID YOU KNOW?

In Hindi, *barasingha* means "twelve points," a reference to the number of branches on a male barasingha deer's antlers.

ASIAN SAVANNA

Home to greater one-horned Asian rhinos, Arabian oryx, Przewalski's wild horses, gaur, and a variety of unusual deer species from Asia, the Asian Savanna can be viewed from select safari tours. Though the savanna is more than 60 acres in size, there are only a couple of places where guests can view this area on foot: from Condor Ridge and Nativescapes Garden. The savanna is filled with boulders that offer numerous hiding places for the animals—especially for some of the more timid deer species, which fare better when they have access to private areas.

Because of their poor eyesight, rhinos tend to be protective and shy.

CART SAFARI *This safari enables guests to view many animals in the Asian Savanna they may not otherwise see at the Park, including Przewalski's horses, gaur (the largest form of wild cattle), greater one-horned Asian rhinos, and a few different types of Asian deer. Visitors board the safari at African Outpost, where they can choose to see either African or Asian animals in their expansive field exhibits.*

DID YOU KNOW?

These equines are best seen by scanning their habitat with binoculars. The habitat is visible from Condor Ridge.

The Przewalski's horse can be pronounced either "sheh-VAL-skee" or "per-zhuh-VAL-skee" or even "PREZ-val-skee." It is also known as the Asiatic wild horse, or the Mongolian wild horse.

The Przewalski's horse is the closest living relative of the domestic horse—but is stocky and short, with a spiky mane like a zebra's. These horses have a light belly and darker back, with one long, dark stripe from the withers to the base of the tail. Unlike their horsey cousins, they don't have a lock of hair on their forehead. They do, however, have ancient roots: thirty-thousand-year-old cave paintings found in Spain and France depict wild horses with the features of the Przewalski's horse.

The Safari Park has a herd of off-exhibit males and a group of females in an enclosure beside the Asian field habitat. Since they don't have to compete for a stallion's attention, these females spend their days nuzzling, engaging in mutual grooming, rolling in the dust, and eating. San Diego Zoo Global participates in the Species Survival Plan (SSP) for the Przewalski's horse. The Park is currently breeding animals to be reintroduced into Kazakhstan.

Arabian Oryx

These strikingly beautiful antelope of the Arabian Peninsula and Sinai Desert have long, straight, and slender horns. The Arabian oryx are well adapted to desert extremes: Their light color reflects the desert heat and sunlight, and they can erect their hair on cold winter mornings to capture warm air in their thick undercoat. Their legs also darken in the winter to attract and absorb more of the sun's heat.

This species became extinct in the wild in the late 1960s, mostly due to hunting. Nine Arabian oryx from private collections in Oman, Kuwait, and Saudi Arabia, as well as from the London Zoo, were moved to the Phoenix Zoo in Arizona. A second breeding group of three oryx from a Saudi Arabian zoo was relocated to the Los Angeles Zoo, and in the 1970s, animals from both of these herds were sent to the Safari Park. These animals, more than 20 in all, were sent back to Oman from 1980 to 1989 in a series of six moves. In 2011, thanks to these collaborative conservation efforts, the oryx was the first animal to be listed as vulnerable on the endangered list after being classified as extinct in the wild.

MISSION CONSERVATION

Most of the Arabian oryx in the wild today are descended from individuals that were born at the Safari Park or were collected from other institutions, brought to the Park, and readied for their return to their native habitat. As of 2018, more than 400 Arabian oryx had been born at the Park, and many of them were reintroduced to Oman and Jordan. Because oryx are naturally flighty, the Park at first moved young oryx that were used to humans. Once the oryx arrived in Oman, they were placed in highly managed areas—surrounded by the desert but cared for much as they had been at the Safari Park. It took years for them to become fully acclimated. Today, their descendants are truly wild again in the deserts of Arabia.

Also known as the Indian rhino, the greater one-horned Asian rhino is native to the swampy areas of northeast India and Nepal. These rhinos have a large head, broad chest, thick legs, poor eyesight, excellent hearing—and a fondness for rolling in the mud. Although they look armor-plated, they are actually covered with a layer of skin that has many folds. Like all rhinos, greater one-horned Asian rhinos are herbivores, eating grasses or leaves, depending on the species. At the San Diego Zoo Safari Park, they are fed hay and high-fiber biscuits.

For ages, rhino horns have been used to treat illnesses, especially fevers. Yet rhino horns are made of keratin and have no healing properties. In some countries, rhinos are being dehorned, a process that removes the valuable horn but leaves the animal alive and well. This minimizes poaching. Efforts to protect these endangered animals have been successful. At the beginning of the 20th century, there were fewer than 200 greater one-horned rhinos in India and Nepal; today, with the help of the International Rhino Foundation, the population has grown to more than 3,550!

MISSION CONSERVATION

San Diego Zoo Global provides support and funding for greater one-horned rhinoceros conservation efforts in India and Nepal. A team from the Safari Park works with the International Rhino Foundation and other partners to translocate wild rhinos from national parks that have large rhino populations to other areas where the species has been depleted and has room to expand. In addition, more than 70 greater one-horned rhinos have been born at the Safari Park, where there are more births of this species than at any other zoo in the world.

Père David's Deer

More than 3,000 years ago, one million Père David's deer roamed the open plains and marshes of China. Over time, the wild herds diminished due to overhunting. In the 19th century, the Emperor of China saved them from extinction, placing the only surviving herd in captivity in Imperial Hunting Park. The deer soon multiplied, and the emperor gifted many of the animals to zoos in Europe.

During the Boxer Rebellion at the turn of the 20th century, the remaining Chinese herd was slaughtered and eaten by soldiers, causing the deer to become extinct in their native land. Fortunately, the deer in Europe were thriving. European zoos worked together to conserve the species and rescue the population. Today, thanks to many conservation efforts, Père David's deer are found in zoos around the globe.

MISSION CONSERVATION

Although Père David's deer were declared extinct in the wild in 2008, the captive populations are stable and do not suffer from genetic problems. In the future, zoos around the world hope to reintroduce these semi-aquatic animals back into their native Chinese habitat.

Tigers have three-inch-long canine teeth and powerful jaws. Tigers typically make a kill once or twice a week, returning to their hidden prey over several days.

TIGER TRAIL

SOME OF THE LARGEST CARNIVORES AT THE SAFARI PARK reside in the Tull Family Tiger Trail. This award-winning, five-acre exhibit—designed to mimic the tigers' Indonesian habitat—gives the Park's group of Sumatran tigers plenty of space to roam. There are ample viewing opportunities for visitors to see the usually elusive cats, including a Log Walk that leads to a large viewing window, a waterfall for the tigers to splash among the rocks and streams, and a deep pool where they show off their swimming prowess both above and below the water.

Tiger Trail, which received top honors from the Association of Zoos and Aquariums (AZA), provides ample space for the Park to breed the critically endangered tigers. The exhibit also educates guests about the Sumatran tigers' plight in the wild, with a pondok, or Indonesian hut, where a conservationist explains how people can help prevent illegal poaching.

With their partially webbed toes, tigers are powerful swimmers. They can often be found relaxing or waiting in ponds, streams, and rivers to ambush their prey.

All tigers have their own unique stripe pattern, and those who observe tigers can identify individuals by their particular stripes. As stalk-and-ambush hunters, tigers are camouflaged in tall grass by their orange, black, and white stripes, which break up their outline as they wait for prey to come near. Tigers also have white spots on the backs of their ears. These may help them find one another, or they may be a way for mothers and cubs to keep one another in sight in the dense forest undergrowth. Some researchers believe the spots are designed to resemble staring eyes to scare predators that may be behind them.

Even though Sumatrans are the smallest tiger subspecies, they are still pretty big cats—about the length of a school cafeteria table! The Safari Park has a small group of critically endangered Sumatran tigers. Keepers scatter treats to encourage foraging behavior and spray scents through the exhibit to stimulate the tigers' olfactory curiosity. Sometimes they even use products from other animals, such as ocelot bedding, rhino dung, or camel hair.

MISSION CONSERVATION

Found on the Indonesian island of Sumatra, critically endangered Sumatran tigers are the last of the Indonesian tigers. They are hunted for their body parts and threatened by habitat loss.

Researchers estimate that fewer than 3,500 tigers exist in the wild, and only about 400 of those are Sumatran. More than 25 tiger cubs have been born at the Safari Park since 1971. The Park participates in the Species Survival Plan (SSP) for the Sumatran tiger. The SSP tracks genetic diversity among zoo tigers and uses the information to pair males and females. Careful breeding helps create a genetic insurance policy for tigers in the wild.

Tigers have large and strong front paws to bring down their prey. Their claws can be pulled inside while they walk, which helps keep them sharp.

LION CAMP

CATCH A GLIMPSE
The Park's pride likes to stalk, pounce, and wrestle with one another along the grassy plain at the top of the hill in Lion Camp.
The lions can also be seen relaxing with each other.

Female cubs usually stay with the pride they were born into, and mothers and daughters may live together for life.

LION CAMP

THE SAFARI PARK'S LION CAMP IS DESIGNED TO BRING VISITORS right into the world of African lions. At one end of Lion Camp is a group of rocks and boulders where the lions can climb, lounge—and stare at guests behind floor-to-ceiling glass. A second part of the habitat is comprised of an open, grassy plain that starts at the top of a hill and slopes gently downward. Visitors can again come eye-to-eye with the lions near the "researchers' tent," giving them a taste of what it would be like to have lions prowling through their camp in Africa!

Lions are the only members of the cat family to have males and females that look distinctly different.

BEHIND THE SCENES

The lions at Safari Park often receive enrichment items. Keepers place interesting scents in Lion Camp, such as wood shavings from the Park's hoofed stock barns or herbs that are rubbed on a rock. Food enrichment can include large blocks of ice that are filled with chunks of meat (called meat-sicles) or whole fish (fish-sicles). Cardboard boxes, palm fronds, feed sacks, and heavy-duty plastic balls make great toys too.

African Lion

*a*n African lion's life is all about sleeping, napping, and resting. In a 24-hour period, lions will have short bursts of intense activity, followed by long bouts of lying around that can total up to 21 hours. These felines are good climbers and often rest in trees, possibly to catch a cool breeze or to get away from flies.

Lions live in prides usually consisting of a dominant male, many females, and their offspring. Living in a pride makes life easier. Hunting as a group means there is a better chance that lions will get food when they need it, and makes it less likely that they will get injured while hunting. Lion researchers have noticed that some activities are "contagious" in prides. One lion will yawn, or groom itself, or roar, setting off a wave of yawning, grooming, or roaring.

Lions and lionesses play different roles in the life of the pride. Lions live in a matriarchal society. The lionesses work together to hunt and rear the cubs. Being smaller and lighter than males, lionesses are more agile and faster. During hunting, smaller females chase the prey toward the center. The larger and heavier lionesses ambush or capture the prey. Lionesses are versatile and can switch hunting jobs depending on which females are hunting that day and what kind of prey is involved.

Lions can survive in extreme drought conditions. In the Kalahari Desert, they often get needed moisture by eating tsamma melons.

It may look like the lionesses do all the work, but the males play an important role. While they do eat more than the lionesses and bring in far less food (they hunt less than 10 percent of the time), males patrol, mark, and guard the pride's territory. Males also guard the cubs while the lionesses are hunting and make sure the cubs get enough food.

It is estimated that there are between 6,000 and 10,000 lions in Africa. Their natural habitat is now only on protected reserves, but lions are doing well in those places. Although there are still enough lions

Cubs born in a pride are twice as likely to survive as cubs born to a lioness on her own.

to provide genetic diversity and prevent inbreeding, lion movement between prides is becoming more limited. Some hunting is still allowed on reserves, and often there are so many lions in such limited territory that rangers put the females on birth control.

The Balloon Safari is modeled after the hot air balloon tours of the Serengeti. This tethered, helium-filled balloon can carry up to 30 people and rise 400 feet, giving riders a panoramic view of the lions, rhinos, giraffes, wildebeest, and gazelles. Tickets are available at the balloon site, and each launch lasts approximately 15 minutes. The best flying conditions are in the early afternoon.

One of the most popular attractions at the Safari Park is Shiley's Cheetah Run, located in Lion Camp. Here, guests can see the fastest land mammal up close, doing what it does best: run! During the presentation, the spotted sprinter races on a straight 330-foot-long track that allows the cheetah to really stretch its legs and reach astounding speeds. In just four seconds, the cheetah goes from zero to about 70 miles per hour while chasing a mechanical lure attached to its favorite toy.

CHEETAH SAFARI
This paid safari provides guests with prime seating for the daily Cheetah Run. Participants can meet animal ambassadors before the run, meet the "runner" cheetah afterward, and talk with the trainer.

The lion's thick mane protects his neck against raking claws during fights with other males for membership and rank in the pride.

AFRICAN PLAINS

Wildebeest calves grow up quickly: they can walk 15 minutes after birth, and they develop horns after just a few weeks.

AFRICAN PLAINS

AFRICAN PLAINS IS AN EXPANSIVE TERRITORY that features several distinct habitats—from desert to savanna to forest to marshland. Each is designed to recreate the animals' habitat in the wild, allowing them to engage in natural behaviors such as courtship and offspring-rearing practices, and herding and dominance behaviors. Here, the animals can mingle with other species that would normally share their habitat. The animals are even close enough to hear the roars of their predators—the lions stationed at Lion Camp—just like they would in the wild.

Many threatened animals call the African Plains home, such as the southern white rhino. The area is also host to large herds of giraffes, cape buffalo, wildebeest, impalas, oryx, and gazelles. In addition, the Plains have a variety of birds, such as East and West African crowned cranes, ostriches, storks, flamingos, and pelicans.

Wild asses are intelligent creatures, with excellent vision and hearing. They would rather run from predators than fight.

Giraffe

The word giraffe is derived from the Arabic *zarafah*, meaning "one who walks swiftly." Giraffes are the only mammals born with horns. Their horns, called ossicones, are comprised of soft cartilage when they are born and harden as they mature. Reaching up to 18 feet, the giraffe is the tallest living land mammal. Giraffes range in weight from 2,000 to 3,000 pounds.

Calves can walk within an hour of birth. When they get a little older, they naturally form a group, called a crèche—a type of kindergarten where they develop physical and social skills through play under the watchful eye of a designated guardian (usually one of the mothers or grandmothers). While the mothers move about feeding, grooming, and socializing, the calves remain clustered together. The youngsters explore their surroundings, taking frequent breaks to check in with their mother for nursing sessions or to munch on leaves.

MISSION CONSERVATION

Giraffes are quietly disappearing because of poaching as well as habitat loss and fragmentation. Experts are calling this a "silent extinction." San Diego Zoo Global works closely with local communities and other partners in Kenya to study and protect giraffes. The Twiga Walinzi, or Giraffe Guards, is comprised of local people who help monitor giraffe populations and manage 120 camera traps.

DID YOU KNOW?

Fossil records show that crowned cranes existed 54 million years ago.

East African crowned cranes are named for the tuft of fine feathers on top of their head. Their distinctive brushlike feathered adornment provides them with the perfect camouflage in the tall grass of their marsh, lakeside, and riverbank habitats. Crowned cranes will spread their wings to show off in dramatic courtship dances. They are monogamous, and pairs preen mutually, especially around their face and neck. When foraging, they will stamp the ground to stir up insects. They also feed on seeds, mollusks, and amphibians.

More than 50 East African crowned cranes have hatched at the Park since 1972. Although the crowned crane itself is not endangered, 11 out of the 15 living crane species are endangered or considered vulnerable. At the Park, if a pair of cranes is not taking care of its eggs, keepers will cross-foster the eggs, giving them to a different pair of birds who are experienced parents—even different species of birds. For cranes living in field habitats that are shared with large mammals, the keepers will put their eggs into incubators so they remain intact. The eggs are replaced with "dummy eggs" to ensure the parents will continue their natural nesting behavior; then, just before hatching, the real eggs are put back in the nest. After hatching, the entire family is taken to another location until the chicks are a bit older.

BEHIND THE SCENES

Although all zebras are wild, the Grevy's zebra is more mellow and social than the two other species. At the Park, the Grevy's zebras even let the keepers enter their habitat. Of course, the keepers park their trucks nearby— just in case.

Endangered Grevy's zebras are the largest of the three zebra species, weighing up to 990 pounds. They have the most delicate striping, with lines that continue all the way to their hooves. Grevy's zebras recognize one another by their unique striping. Their large ears help them listen for danger and even allow them to communicate with one another by pointing in the direction of the concern.

Unlike other female zebras, which live in harems year round, female Grevy's zebras usually move through the males' territory only during breeding season. The Park's herd can be seen from the Africa Tram.

MISSION CONSERVATION

About 2,250 Grevy's zebras remain in the wild, their numbers decimated by loss of habitat and anthrax bacteria outbreaks. San Diego Zoo Global is a member of the Grevy's Zebra Trust and is working with other groups to preserve the population.

Ostrich

The ostrich is the largest and heaviest living bird, reaching heights of eight to nine feet and weighing up to 350 pounds. An ostrich egg is also the single largest cell. Inside the egg, chicks will make calls that the parents answer!

Ostriches have large eyes, providing them with excellent eyesight to scan for danger. Though they are flightless, these birds are fast. Their strides span 12 to 16 feet, and they can reach—and maintain—speeds of up to 45 miles per hour in order to outdistance their predators. Their wings help them balance when running at full speed. It's a myth that ostriches bury their head in the sand when sensing danger. If they can't run away, they simply flop to the ground and lay still. Their lightly colored neck and head blends in with the sand. The Safari Park is assisting with the conservation of the endangered red-necked ostrich in Niger, West Africa.

DID YOU KNOW?

An ostrich's kick is powerful enough to kill a lion!

African Rhino

All rhinoceroses are herbivores, ingesting between 3 to 5 percent of their weight in plant matter each day. There are two kinds of rhinos in Africa: black and white. Black rhinos are browsers that pluck leaves from bushes and low hanging trees with their prehensile, pointed upper lip, while white rhinos are grazers that have wide flat lips and elongated skulls that enable them to eat short grasses. Rhinos have a massive head as well as a keen sense of smell and hearing. They can run approximately 30 miles per hour.

Black rhinos, which are actually brownish gray, are critically endangered; most live on protected, managed game reserves. Southern white rhinos are considered near threatened. In the late 1800s, farmers and hunters killed large numbers of these rhinos in South Africa. Yet thanks to global conservation efforts, their populations have stabilized. Northern white rhinos are among the world's most endangered animals. Currently, there are just two in a secure park in Kenya.

MISSION CONSERVATION

The Safari Park is a world leader in breeding southern white rhinos in a zoo setting—nearly 100 calves have been born at the Park since the early 1970s. However, the second generation of female rhinos born at the Park had low fertility rates. The Institute for Conservation Research discovered that dietary phytoestrogens—chemicals produced by soy and alfalfa—mimicked the hormone estrogen and caused the reproductive issues. Once the rhinos were switched to diets low in phytoestrogens, they started having babies!

Black rhinos use their semi-prehensile, tapered upper lip to pluck leaves from bushes and low trees.

SAFARI NOTES

One female southern white rhino will bond with another female and hang around her—for meals, mud wallows, and naps—for life! Apart from breeding, females mostly associate with their best friend, even bringing one another's calves into their small circle. If they are separated, it can affect their hormones and keep them from successfully breeding.

AFRICAN OUTPOST

The lowland nyala, found in south-eastern Africa, is one of nine species of spiral-horned antelope.

AFRICAN OUTPOST

BAT-EARED FOXES, HORNBILLS, FLAMINGOS, and the heaviest flying bird, the kori bustard, all call the African Outpost home. The cheetah habitat is also here: it overlooks the Park's East Africa field enclosure and is designed to make visitors feel as if they are seeing cheetahs on an African safari.

African Outpost is the starting spot for the Africa Tram and Cart Safari tours. At Okavango Outpost, which is nearby, visitors can dine on sandwiches, salads, kids' meals, and more while overlooking a flamingo lagoon and animal habitats.

Bat-eared foxes eat insects, including termites, which they lick up from the ground. Their large, specialized ears enable them to hear the insects moving around.

BEHIND THE SCENES

Since female cheetahs do not have regular ovulation cycles, it is difficult for the Park keepers to know when to put them together for breeding. Fortunately, researchers have discovered that males make a unique "stutter bark" during the breeding season. Keepers record these stutter barks, manipulate them on the computer so they sound like a stranger's bark, and then play the sounds to the females to help them get "in the mood." Within days, the females begin to show interest in the males.

Long and lanky, cheetahs are uniquely designed to run very fast for fairly short distances, allowing them to catch prey that other big cats find elusive. They have a flexible spine that allows their front legs to stretch far forward on each stride, and their claws are hard and sharp like cleats, giving them great traction to catch their 20-foot strides. As the fastest land mammal on earth, they can reach speeds up to 70 miles per hour.

Just like cheetahs run fast, they must also eat fast, since leopards, lions, and hyenas will steal their food if given the chance. Because these endangered animals aren't strong enough to hide or guard their catch, they must kill more often, making them expend more energy than other big cats.

Cheetahs are vocal, making unique, birdlike sounds called "chirrups" when they're excited. Mothers use the same sound to call their cubs. Cheetahs purr, growl, snarl, hiss, cough, moan, and bleat, but they cannot roar like lions or tigers do.

Cubs live with their mother for about 18 months but often become prey to lions, leopards, and hyenas. To protect her cubs, a mother moves them frequently.

Ground Hornbill

With dark eyes, long eyelashes made of modified feathers, and an almost comically large, curved bill, hornbills are among nature's most unusual birds. These birds range from small (the size of a pigeon) to large (having a six-foot wingspan). They are easily distinguishable from other birds by a special body part atop their bill called a casque, a hollow structure made out of keratin. Researchers believe that this structure acts as a vibrating chamber to make their voice louder. Their calls range from the deep booming sounds they make as they begin foraging for food to brays, toots, bellows, and cackles.

The African Outpost is home to Abyssinian (northern) ground hornbills. Ground hornbills are able to fly, but they prefer to walk or run. The ground hornbills are the largest of the species, with black feathers on their body and primary white feathers on their wings— seen only when they are in flight. Both species patrol their territory on foot in groups of up to a dozen individuals. Northern ground hornbills eat mice. They also eat other rodents, frogs, and even venomous snakes, which they catch by using their long bill as tongs, keeping the rest of their body out of harm's way.

DID YOU KNOW?

In 1972, the San Diego Zoo Safari Park produced the first Abyssinian (northern) ground hornbill chick to be born in a zoo. The chick's parents lived to be more than 50 years old and had 50 more offspring.

Colobus Monkey

With their thick black and white fur, colobus monkeys are among the world's most distinctive primates. Native to Central Africa, they spend most of their time in the upper part of the forest canopy. Their digestive system is similar to a cow's, with a three-part stomach that enables them to digest large amounts of leaves.

Unlike most primates, colobus monkeys do not have thumbs. Instead, they use their four fingers to grip the branches as they move quickly through the trees. They are known to leap great distances to avoid predators and use branches as springboards to jump into the air. Their mane and tail are thought to act as a parachute that slows them before they grab the next branch.

Colobus monkeys live in family groups consisting of one male, several females, and their offspring. The females take shared roles in raising the babies, helping to maintain the cohesion of the group.

Flamingos' feathers aren't naturally pink. Their pink or reddish color comes from the rich sources of carotenoid pigments in the algae and small crustaceans that they eat. At the Safari Park, the flamingos are fed a special pellet diet that includes a pigment that helps maintain their beautiful color. Unlike many African animals that rely on their coloring to help them blend into their surroundings, flamingos don't have to worry much about predators. They tend to live in inhospitable places where the lagoons are pretty bare of vegetation, so few other birds or animals come there.

Flamingos have very distinctive eating habits. Using their long legs, they wade into deep water to look for food. Then they hold their bill upside down in the water and feed by sucking in water and mud at the front of their bill and pumping it out at the sides. Fringed plates in their bill called lamellae act like filters, trapping shrimp and other small water creatures for them to eat.

SAFARI NOTES

Flamingos live in groups that may be tens of thousands in number. They usually fly in large flocks, using a variety of formations that help them take advantage of the wind patterns. In flight, flamingos are quite distinctive, flapping their wings almost continuously with their long neck stretched out in front and equally long legs trailing behind.

Flamingos build their nests out of mud, using their bill to draw the mud toward their feet. Their nests are about 12 inches high—tall enough to protect the egg from flooding and to keep it cool, if needed. Flamingos lay a single large egg, which is incubated by both parents.

At hatching, flamingo chicks have gray down feathers, straight, pink bills, and swollen pink legs, both of which turn black within a week. After hatching, chicks stay in the nest for five to 12 days. During this time, they are fed "crop milk," which comes from their parents' upper digestive tracts. Both males and females can feed chicks this way, and other flamingos can act as foster-feeders. Researchers believe the begging calls of hungry chicks help to stimulate the secretion of milk.

Chicks and their parents, like these lesser flamingos, recognize one another through their distinctive calls.

The Park has the largest flock of greater flamingos in the United States at around 150 birds.

Male giant elands measure up to 11 feet long. They break off branches for food with their spiral horns.

AFRICAN WOODS

AFRICAN WOODS INCLUDES A WINDING PATH with views of forest animals like elusive okapis, graceful gerenuks, striking bonteboks, and the largest antelope in Africa—the giant eland. There is also an array of bird species like vultures, cranes, and secretary birds, and small antelope such as the yellow-backed duiker. With trails that lead through gentle terrain, African Woods offers many places to sit beneath trees and appreciate the flora and fauna of Africa. It also includes the immersive Lemur Walk, where visitors can stroll through the lemurs' habitat and watch the primates socialize, groom, jump, climb, and sunbathe. Nearby is the Jungle Gym play area for families, which is adjacent to the Samburu Terrace dining facility.

Okapi can travel up to one-half mile each day in search of food. They eat 40 to 65 pounds of leaves, twigs, and fruits each day.

Okapi

BEHIND THE SCENES

Researchers used to believe that okapis were non-vocal. However, studies have shown that they are in fact very talkative creatures. Their calls are just so low in frequency that humans cannot hear them. To study okapis, Park keepers use highly sensitive microphones, digital recording equipment, and specialized software to record the calls and push these sounds into auditory ranges that humans can hear.

With their white-and-black striped hindquarters and front legs, okapis (pronounced oh-cop-ee) look like they are related to zebras. In reality, they are the only living relatives of the giraffe. Like giraffes, okapis have large, upright ears, which catch even slight sounds. They also have a long, dark prehensile tongue to help them strip buds and young leaves from the understory brush of the rainforest.

Okapis are difficult to find in the wild; their natural habitat is the Ituri Forest, a dense rainforest in Central Africa. They are quite wary, and their highly developed hearing alerts them to run when they hear humans in the distance. In fact, while natives of the Ituri Forest were familiar with okapis, scientists did not discover them until 1900. The Safari Park has one of the most successful breeding programs for okapis: more than three dozen calves have been born here.

Baby okapis can stand up within 30 minutes of birth. Mothers hide their newborn calves in one spot, returning regularly to nurse.

Secretary Bird

These African birds of prey look like cranes but act more like eagles. In fact, secretary birds are so unique—both in looks and how they capture prey—that they're in their own scientific family.

Secretary birds are the tallest birds of prey and also the most terrestrial. They stalk reptiles, insects, and small mammals on the ground. There are two theories as to why they are called "secretary birds." Some people say their long tail feathers and head plumes reminded early biologists of a legal secretary wearing a gray tailcoat with a quill pen tucked behind his ear. The more likely theory is that the word "secretary" derives from an Arabic term meaning "hunter-bird." The Park has produced more chicks than any zoo in North America.

Lemur

Lemurs are considered the world's most endangered group of mammals. They are found in only one area on Earth—Madagascar and the nearby Comoro Islands. There are more than 100 species of lemurs. Most lemurs spend their time up in the trees, resting, sleeping, feeding, and even giving birth, but ring-tailed lemurs also spend a good portion of their day on the ground. These social animals communicate through scent marking and vocalization. Male ring-tailed lemurs have stink fights by rubbing their wrist scent glands all over their tail, then waving it in front of each other's face. These lemurs also use their ringed tail for communication—holding it up so the others can see where they are in the forest.

Giant elands are the world's largest species of antelope. Found in the woodlands and savannas of West, Central, and East Africa, they are also known as Lord Derby's eland, named in honor of the 13th Earl of Derby, who had a large private zoo on the grounds of his home in 19th century England. These antelope have spiraling horns that can reach close to four feet long. The twisting is a result of a growth pulse—controlled by genetics—in which the horn material grows faster and thinner at certain times, and then slower and thicker at other times.

Giant elands feed on leaves and fruits. These nocturnal animals use their long horns to pull down branches of certain trees and twist their head vigorously to shake out any fruit. Their horns are also useful for digging up thick-leaved plants, bulbs, roots, melons, and onions. Despite their large size—they are about five feet tall at the shoulder, 11 feet long, and can weigh as much as 2,000 pounds—giant elands are quite agile. They can leap higher than five feet in the air when necessary!

The growth rate for young giant elands is very rapid due to their mothers' rich milk.

Egyptian Vulture

Many people have negative connotations when it comes to vultures. But only modern societies are hostile toward these scavenging birds. In fact, most ancient civilizations had a neutral or positive attitude about them.

DID YOU KNOW?

Vultures are an important part of our ecosystem—they may prevent the spread of disease by disposing of animal carcasses.

Several types of vultures inhabit the Safari Park, including Egyptian vultures. Considered Old World vultures, Egyptian vultures look like their eagle and hawk relatives with their large, grasping talons. They build nests made of sticks on rocky platforms. Like other vultures, Egyptian vultures have their own flair for getting their food—breaking open ostrich eggs by dropping stones on them, sometimes repeatedly until the egg cracks.

These endangered antelope, which feed on short grasses, are territorial. Bonteboks live in groups consisting of one male, several females, and their offspring. Bachelors form their own herds.

At one time, these striking brown and white antelope were considered pests. By 1830, South African colonists had almost hunted them to extinction. Today, bonteboks can be found in a few preserves in South Africa as well as in various zoos.

Male bonteboks mark their territory with special scent glands, urine, and dung piles. Females wander from one territory to another.

The name gerenuk (pronounced with a hard "g") comes from the Somali word *garanug*, which means "giraffe-necked." Like giraffes, gerenuks use their long neck and long legs to reach the best browse (food) overhead. The gerenuks at the Park are fed an herbivore pellet diet, but the keepers also hang browse so the animals can feed in their usual way. Native to arid areas in northeastern Africa, reddish-brown gerenuks get most of their water from their food.

Males have long, ringed horns that reach 14 to 17 inches, and both sexes have several scent glands. One of these is found in front of each eye—a pitlike opening called a preorbital gland. With their scent glands, gerenuks secrete fluid on grass, twigs, and even other gerenuks to mark their territory.

The generuks' range has shrunk over many decades. Although their populations are stable in protected areas, their numbers continue to decline in locations where they are hunted for their hide.

BEHIND THE SCENES

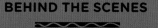

The keepers at the Park trained the gerenuks to stand upright on cue so they could perform a blood draw just above the front hoof when necessary. Gerenuks are extremely shy animals. To facilitate human contact, Park keepers hung browse on a gate and stood near it while the animals ate. Over time, the keepers moved closer until they could hold the branch and have the gerenuks eat from it. Now, some of the gerenuks will eat out of the keepers' hands.

Baby animals that need a helping hand from human caretakers—like this wallaby joey—are raised at the Animal Care Center in Nairobi Village.

NAIROBI VILLAGE

SURROUNDED BY PATHS AND WOODEN WALKWAYS, Nairobi Village simulates a Congo fishing village with its picturesque waterfall, thatched huts, raised walkways, and lagoon. Many of the Park's wildlife ambassadors in the Animal Encounters program go for walks with their trainers around the village. Animals exhibited here include the critically endangered Rodrigues fruit bats, warthogs, and red-knobbed hornbills.

Several popular places to visit in the Village include Nairobi Station, an interactive experience, and the Petting Kraal, where children can pet three types of exotic African goats. The Benbough Amphitheater, which features the Frequent Flyers bird show, is located nearby.

The Petting Kraal contains pygmy goats, Boer goats, and Nubian goats that are just the right size for children to pet and sometimes brush.

Mombasa Lagoon is a peaceful watering hole that is home to pelicans, storks, shoebills, and ducks, along with migratory birds like herons and egrets. About 150 birds, representing 20 to 25 species, live here. On one side of the lagoon are meerkats, warthogs, and tiny dik-dik antelope. On the other side are bee-eater birds and Gorilla Forest.

A fishing village dominates the north end of the lagoon. It features hand-woven, conical traps similar to those used by villagers who fish the Congo River. Scattered around the area are walkways to several animal habitats and fun spots for children to explore. For example, kids can climb into a replica of an aardvark's den or hop on springy, lifelike lily pads.

CATCH A GLIMPSE

Guests can climb up the tower located in Mombasa Lagoon for a real bird's-eye view of Nairobi Village and the surrounding lagoon.

FLIGHTLINE SAFARI

This safari enables participants to soar for two-thirds of a mile over the Park. Guests are first given a practice run before heading to the main Flightline, where they land near the Park's campground at Kilima Point.

Bat wings have the same bones as the fingers on a human hand. A thin, strong membrane spreads across these bones like the fabric and ribs of an umbrella.

Most bats take off by dropping from a hanging position, and many can't take off from the ground. Bats in flight use echolocation—which works similar to sonar—to hunt for insects at night. Bats are not blind, but most have better night vision than day vision. They see in black, white, and shades of gray.

Some people think bats are bloodsuckers that fly into people's hair and carry rabies. In fact, they are extremely useful to humans. Bats are responsible for pollinating flowers, cacti, and trees, including avocados, bananas, breadfruit, dates, figs, mangoes, and peaches. They spread seeds so plants grow in new areas. Many species live together by the millions and can eat half their weight in insects each night—including thousands of mosquitoes—so they help control large numbers of pests that harm crops and spread disease. Their droppings even have microorganisms that may contain important medical uses for humans.

MISSION CONSERVATION

More than 60 species of bats are endangered, including the critically endangered Rodrigues fruit bat, found only on the island of Rodrigues in the Indian Ocean. These bats use their  excellent sense of sight and smell to find ripe fruit to eat. The Safari Park houses a group of Rodrigues fruit bats in a temperature-controlled habitat near Nairobi Station. The Park participates in the Species Survival Plan (SSP) for the Rodrigues fruit bat and regularly contributes to the ongoing preservation efforts for the species.

Shoebill Stork

Shoebill storks stand perfectly still for long periods in marshes, waiting for a fish or frog to come by. These birds often hold their wings out to either side as they wait, which creates shade and draws fish closer. Then they lunge forward and snap up their prey in their wide bill.

Shoebill storks build nests on the ground rather than in trees. Each breeding season, females normally lay one to three rough-surfaced, white eggs. Both parents then care for their chicks, teaching them how to eat by holding up their food. Chicks have to reach out, grab the food, and swallow the whole creature by themselves.

Shoebills are considered vulnerable in their habitat of east-central Africa. Their numbers are declining, with approximately 8,000 left in the wild; only a dozen or so are in a zoo setting. The Safari Park has an off-exhibit breeding aviary to help them bolster the population. One pair lives on an island in Mombasa Lagoon.

SAFARI NOTES

Although shoebills are usually silent, solitary creatures, they do use their massive beak to communicate with one another by "bill-clattering." Young shoebills make a hiccupping sound when they're hungry for food.

JUNGLE ROPES SAFARI

On the Jungle Ropes Safari, guests can decide how much they want to challenge themselves. Three different trails, from beginner to advanced, provide plenty of options for maneuvering through the ropes courses in the treetops.

CATCH A GLIMPSE

Look who's talking in Nairobi Station: it's Robert the Zebra, a funny and interactive digital puppet. Robert chats with kids and adults, sharing what it's like to be a zebra, and asking visitors to answer his questions.

As visitors enter Nairobi Station, a sign indicates that they have entered a wildlife waystation at the Equator in Kenya. Inside this interactive area, guests can see animals such as shy fennec foxes, a tenerec, a massive African bullfrog, and more. Many of the creatures in this area are animal ambassadors, brought out at various times during the day to give guests a closer look. Friendly naturalists share stories about the animals and answer questions. Nairobi Station also includes an African playground with huts and activities that give kids a glimpse into village life by allowing them to carry water on their head and play drums.

DID YOU KNOW?

Dik-diks have a long nose—an adaptation that helps them to live in the arid bush regions of eastern and southwestern Africa. The airflow and evaporation in their mucus membranes cool their blood, which then recirculates through their body.

Dik-diks are a type of dwarf antelope weighing up to 12 pounds and standing about 14 inches tall. They live in the dry brush and grassland regions of eastern and southwestern Africa, eating green grass, leaves, roots, and fruit. Dik-diks can survive for long periods of time without water, getting most of the moisture they need from their diet.

Dik-diks are usually monogamous and live with their mate and their young in well-defined territories. Female dik-diks are known for their alarm calls, but both males and females make shrill whistling sounds. When trouble comes, the female and her offspring will either hide or join the male to mob the predator.

Warthog

Warthogs are remarkable for their strength, intelligence, and flexibility. Unlike many of their African counterparts, they are not endangered because they are so skilled at adapting to new threats. For example, most warthogs like to forage at sunrise and sunset, but if they live in an area where people hunt them, they switch to foraging at night. Males, called boars, have the most obvious "warts," which are actually thick skin growths on their face. The boars ram each other with their head and blunt upper tusks during breeding season to see who is the most powerful. Their warts act as pads to cushion the blows, so they rarely injure each other.

Lorikeet Landing

The interior of Lorikeet Landing is modeled after the rainforests of Australia and New Guinea, the natural habitat of the lorikeet. These birds are also known as brush-tongued parrots because their tongue is specially adapted to extract nectar and pollen from flowers. They are among nature's most beautiful birds, with feathers almost every color of the rainbow.

In this aviary, lorikeets swoop down to enjoy nectar offered by guests. Entrance to the exhibit is free; lorikeet food is available for purchase. The birds have been specially trained to overcome their natural fear of humans, and they aren't shy when it comes to feeding: several birds may land on a guest's arm, head, or shoulders at one time!

GORILLA FOREST

Although gorillas have no natural enemies or predators, they are endangered. Humans have hunted them for bushmeat and destroyed much of their habitat.

In Africa, gorillas usually don't stay in the same place for more than a day. Each morning, the silverback, or eldest male, leads his troop to a new area where food is plentiful. After a morning of munching, each adult gathers leaves, twigs, and branches to make a day nest for resting while the youngsters play. After their nap, the gorillas will eat again until bedtime, when they make yet another nest for a good night's sleep.

GORILLA FOREST

IN GORILLA FOREST, GUESTS CAN WATCH a troop of western lowland gorillas—and those gorillas will watch right back. Most people find gorillas fascinating to observe. With their animated gestures, opposable thumbs, and similar DNA, they share many characteristics with humans. Gorilla Forest invites visitors to explore these similarities through interactive features that include impressions of a gorilla's hand and foot; a life-size diagram comparing a gorilla and a human; and a sound display that includes the noises gorillas make when they're feeding, threatening one another, or playing.

Near the gorillas, visitors can admire stunning birds in Hidden Jungle, an aviary with an abundance of tropical plants. Hidden Jungle is the site of one of the Park's most popular seasonal attractions—Butterfly Jungle, where thousands of butterflies fill the aviary each spring. The Bird Show Amphitheater is also nearby. There, the Park's clever, trained birds participate in dazzling demonstrations.

Guests can watch birds of various species show off their flying talents during the Frequent Flyers bird show, with many soaring above the audience.

Gorilla

Gorillas are the largest of all primates—the group of animals that includes monkeys, lemurs, orangutans, chimpanzees, and humans. They are peaceful, family-oriented, plant-eating animals. Gorillas also love to eat. Adult males consume up to 40 pounds of leaves, stems, fruits, seeds, and roots each day. Their large stomach can hold the bulky food, and their strong jaws help them chew tough stems. The Safari Park's gorillas are offered a variety of seasonal fruits and vegetables, plus banana and ficus leaves.

Each troop is made up of 5 to 30 gorillas, led by a strong, experienced male known as a silverback. The silverback is responsible for the safety and well-being of the members of his troop. He makes all the decisions, such as where the troop will travel each day, when they will stop to eat or rest, and where they will spend the night.

No two gorilla noses are alike. In the wild, researchers take close-up photos of each gorilla's face to help identify individuals.

Hidden Jungle

CATCH A GLIMPSE

In the Park's Hidden Jungle are species like African pygmy geese, black-cheeked lovebirds (pictured), African fire finches, speckled mousebirds, purple-crested turacos, magpie manikins, and lavender waxbills.

Hidden Jungle is modeled after a tropical rainforest. Often, the wildlife in a tropical rainforest is hard to see, but Hidden Jungle's climate-controlled environment allows visitors to spot numerous delicate and fascinating tropical birds and plants. The trek begins in an earthen crevasse beneath the rain forest floor. There, tree roots snake down the mud walls from the world above. Continuing along the path are the understory and canopy layers of the forest, which has foliage in every shade of green, as well as African birds like the paradise whydah. Other colorful birds, such as the pink pigeon, purple grenadier, and blue-capped cordon bleu, also inhabit this jungle.

Each spring, Hidden Jungle gets an added dose of color during the Park's Butterfly Jungle event. Here, thousands of colorful butterflies hatch and fly through the habitat, adorning orchids, bromeliads, lantana blossoms, and even guests!

Near the gorillas is an aviary of remarkable birds with a specialized skill. They eat bees! But bee-eaters not only eat bees, they also feed on wasps, ants, and butterflies, which they catch in mid-air by diving swiftly and gracefully from their high perch. Bee-eaters have developed a fascinating technique for removing their prey's stingers and venom. With the wriggling bee in their narrow, pointed beak, bee-eaters find a perch of suitable branches. Then they strike the insect repeatedly against their perch to kill it and rub it against the branch to expel its stinger and venom.

Bee-eaters have an interesting social structure that includes "helpers"—juvenile or non-breeding birds in the colony that aid the breeding pairs in raising their chicks. Helpers are often relatives of the breeding pairs. The system helps to raise more chicks successfully this way, and the helpers learn how to raise their own chicks some-day. With more than 60 hatches in the habitat, the Safari Park has the most prolific breeding colony of bee-eaters in North America.

Bee-eaters follow large mammals and terrestrial birds like ostriches, bustards (left), and storks, which stir up insects as they move around.

Water Wise Garden

DID YOU KNOW?

It's easy to save water at home. Try adjusting your lawn mower to a higher setting. A taller lawn shades roots and holds soil moisture better. Another tip is to water your plants for longer periods less often. This conserves water and makes plants root more deeply and become more drought tolerant.

The Water Wise Garden is a good model for gardeners who want to cultivate drought-resistant plants. The Park recycles 100 percent of its wastewater. Used water goes through the on-site water treatment plant instead of the municipal sewer system and then irrigates the Park's field habitats.

Around the landscapes are layers of mulch. Mulch helps prevent water from evaporating; controls erosion by creating an extra barrier between the soil and elements; improves soil structure; and keeps roots cool in the summer and warm in the winter. Mulch—including gravel, decorative and shredded bark, and compost—can be found at any local nursery or home improvement center.

The Safari Park also uses a drip irrigation system that delivers water only where it's needed—at the plant's roots. Choosing the right plants also saves water. Since the Safari Park is located in an arid climate, horticulturists have chosen many "xeriscape" plants with special roots, stems, and leaves. All these methods help a little water go a long way.

Very little is known about Andean bears—also called spectacled bears—in the wild, as they are shy and tend to avoid humans. San Diego Zoo Global researchers in Peru are using camera traps to study these bears, which are facing many threats in their South American habitats.

MISSION CONSERVATION

SAN DIEGO ZOO GLOBAL IS LEADING THE FIGHT AGAINST the extinction of species and habitats worldwide by uniting our expertise in animal care and conservation science with our dedication to inspiring in people a passion for nature.

This not-for-profit organization operates the San Diego Zoo, the San Diego Zoo Safari Park, and the San Diego Zoo Institute for Conservation Research, one of the largest zoo-based research centers in the world. Staff members on all campuses develop, gather, increase, and share knowledge that is vital for the establishment of self-sustaining wildlife populations. This work takes place on grounds at the Zoo, the Park, the Arnold and Mabel Beckman Center for Conservation Research, and through 140 conservation projects in nearly 45 countries on six continents. Some of our biggest success stories have been working to preserve the population of the California condor, establishing the science behind successful rhino breeding, and unlocking and discovering the genome sequence of some of the great apes.

The Safari Park is the foremost breeding facility in the world for the endangered greater one-horned Asian rhino.

San Diego Zoo Global has the largest membership base of any zoo in the world, with more than 430,000 members, including 100,000 child members of the San Diego Zoo Kids Club. In 2012, the San Diego Zoo Global Wildlife Conservancy was launched to generate support for SDZG's worldwide conservation efforts. At more than 6,000 monthly donors strong, these Wildlife Heroes are the heartbeat of everything we do at SDZG. When people join our monthly donor program, they contribute to wildlife conservation efforts around the world and become part of an online global community leading the fight to end extinction. For more information about the Wildlife Conservancy, visit endextinction.org.

DID YOU KNOW?

In addition to housing thousands of plant and animal specimens, the Safari Park also has one of the world's largest "frozen zoos," with thousands of egg and sperm samples from both endangered and non-threatened animals.

As of 2018, the population of California condors had grown to nearly 500, including 300 condors living in the wild.

To address the challenges faced by cheetahs breeding in captivity, the Safari Park keeps males and females separated until mating season and plays sounds of males to help females "get in the mood."

San Diego Zoo Global has the most successful rhino breeding program of its kind in the world. All types of rhinos are critically endangered, but the northern white rhino has suffered most of all. Decades of poaching have left just two females on Earth, and neither animal is fertile. But as part of our vision to lead the fight against extinction, we have a plan to try to bring northern white rhinos back.

In 2015, we built the Nikita Kahn Rhino Rescue Center at the San Diego Zoo Safari Park. This one-of-a-kind sanctuary is dedicated to the conservation and reproduction of white rhinos. Here, our goal is to develop and perfect assisted reproductive technologies for rhinos, including artificial insemination, in vitro fertilization, and embryo transfer.

It's a complicated endeavor, as little is known about the physiology of female white rhino reproduction. Currently, the center is working on artificial insemination techniques, starting with southern white rhino calves. In May 2018, one of the center's six rhinos, Victoria, became

Keepers work closely with the rhinos to build positive relationships with them. The rhinos voluntarily walk into chutes for medical procedures, including veterinary exams and artificial insemination.

pregnant—making her the first rhino in SDZG's history to become pregnant through artificial insemination.

In addition to bolstering the population of southern white rhinos, we hope to eventually make all six southern white rhinos at the Rhino Rescue Center surrogate moms to northern white rhino calves (with help from cutting-edge technologies and our Frozen Zoo®). That could be the answer to saving the northern white rhino from certain extinction.

ABOUT THE SAN DIEGO ZOO

The San Diego Zoo's Conrad Prebys Polar Bear Plunge includes a trio of polar bears that like to swim up to the glass, showing off their playful, acrobatic skills in the pool.

ABOUT THE SAN DIEGO ZOO

LOCATED JUST NORTH OF DOWNTOWN SAN DIEGO IN BALBOA PARK, the world-famous San Diego Zoo cares for more than 3,700 rare and endangered animals representing more than 650 species and subspecies. The Zoo is built on 100 acres of lush canyons and mesas, with many landscaped pathways leading through bioclimatic zones and into aviaries. The Zoo also cultivates a prominent botanical collection with more than 700,000 exotic plants. Here, giant pandas munch on bundles of bamboo, Queensland koalas nestle into eucalyptus trees, polar bears swim through a summer tundra habitat, and one of the nation's largest collections of birds flies through numerous aviaries dense with fern trees and blooming jacaranda.

The San Diego Zoo received its first koalas in 1925. Today, the Zoo is home to the largest koala colony outside of Australia. The koalas—and many other Aussie animals—live in the Conrad Prebys Australian Outback exhibit.

The San Diego Zoo is more than 100 years old. It was founded by a local physician, Dr. Harry Wegeforth, in 1916 when he heard lions roaring as he was driving near the Panama-California International Exposition in Balboa Park. He turned to his brother Paul, who was with him, and said, "Wouldn't it be splendid if San Diego had a zoo? You know, I think I'll start one." A few weeks later, he established the San Diego Zoo with the roaring lions and other animals that had been exhibited at the Exposition.

Since then, the San Diego Zoo has become a world leader in animal husbandry and veterinary care, natural environments for its animal residents, and conservation efforts around the globe. The Zoo is renowned for its botanical collection, education programs, and community outreach efforts, including San Diego Zoo Kids channel, which features closed-circuit television programming about animals. The channel airs in children's hospitals and Ronald McDonald Houses around the world.

The newest area of the Zoo is Conrad Prebys Africa Rocks, which highlights six different African habitats ranging from savanna to seashore. Some of the animals featured include African penguins, Hamadryas baboons, leopards, several species of lemur, dwarf crocodiles, and vervet monkeys.

Africa Rocks includes a growing flock of endangered African penguins. Since 1990, their population in the wild has declined by 60 percent.

Orangutan youngsters stay with their mother until they're seven or eight years old and fully weaned. Thirty orangutans have been born at the Zoo since the first ones arrived in 1928.

The 1,800-acre San Diego Zoo Safari Park (historically referred to as the Wild Animal Park) includes an 800-acre native species reserve and thousands of rare and endangered animals and plants. The Safari Park is run by the nonprofit San Diego Zoo Global (SDZG), which also operates the San Diego Zoo and the San Diego Zoo Institute for Conservation Research. SDZG focuses on conservation and research work around the globe, educates millions of individuals each year about wildlife, and maintains accredited horticultural, animal, library, and photo collections. Conservation and science efforts are supported in part by the Foundation of San Diego Zoo Global.

San Diego Zoo Global Mission:
To save species worldwide by uniting our expertise in animal care and conservation science with our dedication to inspiring passion for nature.

San Diego Zoo Global Vision:
To lead the fight against extinction.

To learn more about the San Diego Zoo Safari Park or to plan a visit and purchase tickets, visit sdzsafaripark.org or call 619-718-3000 or toll free 800-407-9534.

San Diego Zoo Safari Park
15500 San Pasqual Valley Road
Escondido, CA 92027-7017
760-747-8702

Photos © San Diego Zoo Global.

San Diego Zoo Safari Park: Official Guidebook was developed by Beckon Books in association with San Diego Zoo Global Press. Beckon develops and publishes custom books for leading cultural attractions, corporations, and nonprofit organizations. Beckon Books is an imprint of Southwestern Publishing Group, Inc., 2451 Atrium Way, Nashville, Tennessee, 37214. Southwestern Publishing Group, Inc., is a wholly owned subsidiary of Southwestern, Inc., Nashville, Tennessee.

Christopher G. Capen, *President, Southwestern Publishing Group*
Betsy Holt, *Publisher, Beckon Books*
Kristin Connelly, *Managing Editor, Southwestern Publishing Group*
Kristin Stephany, *Director of Partner Development, Southwestern Publishing Group*
Monika Stout, *Design/Production*
swpublishinggroup.com
800-358-0560

ISBN: 978-1-935442-17-2
Printed in China
10 9 8 7 6 5 4